Bad Secrets!

No, not for me!

Written by Keesha L. Pittman

Illustrations by Windel Eborlas

AuthorHouse™
1663 Liberty Drive
Bloomington, IN 47403
www.authorhouse.com
Phone: 833-262-8899

Because of the dynamic nature of the Internet, any web addresses or links contained in this book may have changed since publication and may no longer be valid. The views expressed in this work are solely those of the author and do not necessarily reflect the views of the publisher, and the publisher hereby disclaims any responsibility for them.

Any people depicted in stock imagery provided by Getty Images are models, and such images are being used for illustrative purposes only.
Certain stock imagery © Getty Images.

Interior Image Credit: Windel Eborlas

This book is printed on acid-free paper.

ISBN: 979-8-8230-1255-3 (sc)
ISBN: 979-8-8230-1257-7 (hc)
ISBN: 979-8-8230-1256-0 (e)

Library of Congress Control Number: 2023914188

Print information available on the last page.

Published by AuthorHouse 08/16/2023

authorHOUSE®

Bad Secrets!

No, not for me!

Parents and Guardians:

Molestation and sexual abuse are important topics to discuss with your children. It is difficult to think about or discuss; however, it brings awareness to help avoid or stop it.

Some children have been taught that bad people are only strangers that look or act scary. Let's not forget, bad people may be someone that a child may know as well.

Children should never judge a book by its cover. Also, they should never keep secrets that can hurt them.

Let's talk about bad secrets for awareness and stop it from entering our lives!

There are many people all
around the world.

Some people you may know and
some people you may not know.

They may be tall or short. They
may be funny or not so funny.

They may even wear nice
or not so nice clothes.

There are some good and bad people too.

Some bad people may be in your family or place of worship. They could be a friend, coach, teacher, or someone else at school.

Anyone!

A bad person may offer you money, candy, toys, or something else that you may like.

They may ask you for help finding something in or near their car or house. They will do anything to get your attention and trust.

The way someone looks on the outside does not always make them nice and friendly on the inside.

Some bad people may act nice or pretend to be your friend so that you can trust them.

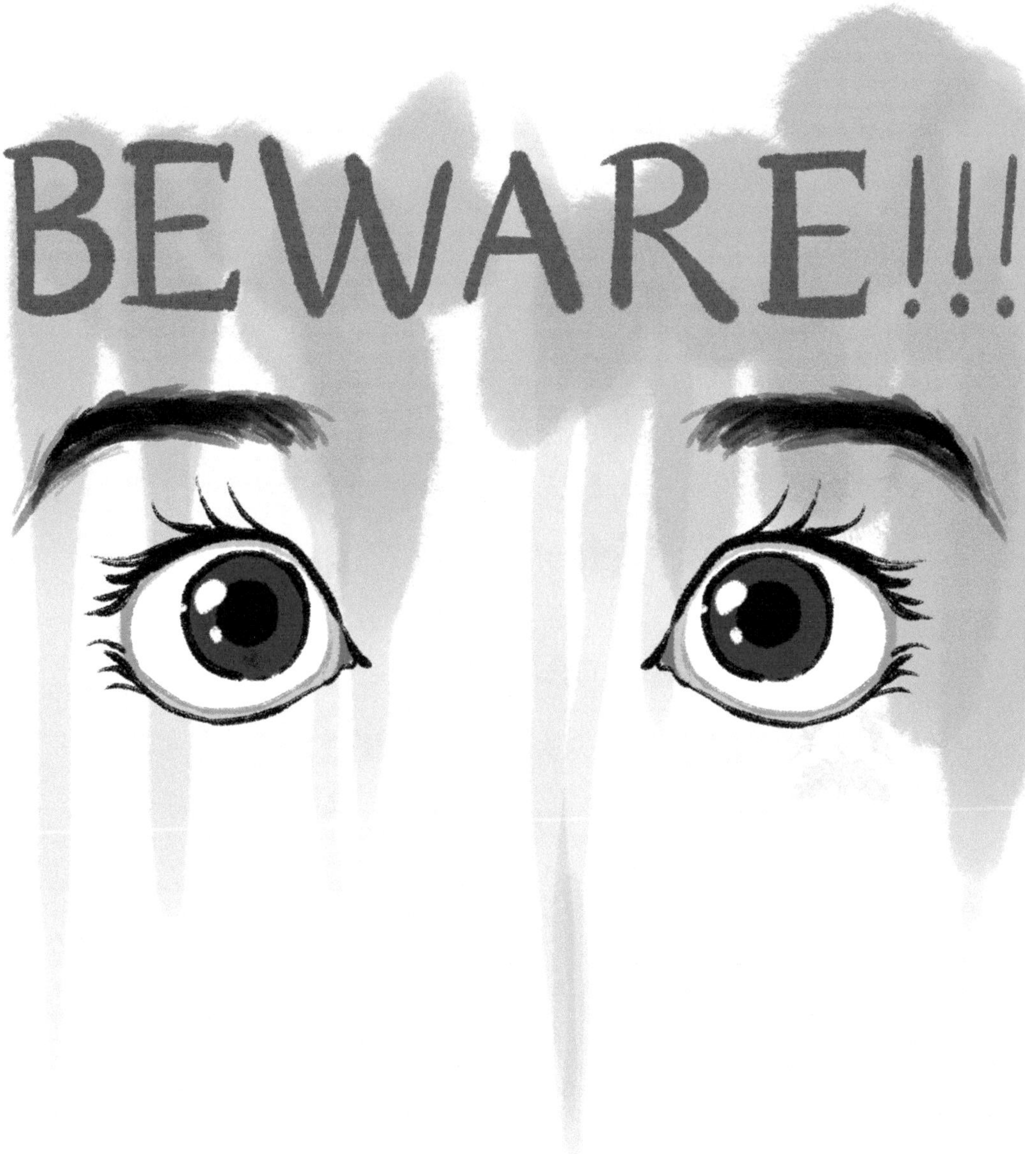
BEWARE!!!

You may not know what they want to do
to you until you are alone with them.

They may try bad things when
you are alone with them.

They may try bad things that they
would never do around other people
who love and care about you.

That is because they know
that it is bad and wrong.

Boys and girls are born with
many body parts.

Some body parts are private
and should never be touched in
a bad, wrong, or hurtful way.

Your private body parts are always
covered when you go outside. They
are not out for everyone to see like
your face, eyes, nose, and ears.

Some people use different names for
their private body parts. They are usually
called penis, vagina, chest, and behind.

You can choose other names for
your private body parts that you
are more comfortable saying.

A bad person may tell you not to
tell anyone that they touched your
private body parts or hurt you.

They may tell you to keep it a secret.

They may even say that nobody
will believe you or they will hurt
you if you tell anyone.

POLICE

16

Never keep it a secret! Tell a person that you can trust right away! You can also call the police by dialing 911 on your phone.

If not, it can happen again or maybe something worse.

It is not easy for boys and girls
to talk about someone that is
touching their private body parts.

They may be scared or embarrassed.

If it happens to you, it is not
your fault! You are a child!

Find a person that you can
trust and can talk to.

Pick a *special word or hand sign*
only known between you and a
person that you can trust.

It can be used to quickly tell
them that you need help.

Remember:

A bad person can be anyone!

Let's say it again and loud this time!

A BAD PERSON CAN BE ANYONE!!!!!

It can be a person that you know or do not know.

Be careful and pay attention.

PLEASE MAKE THIS PROMISE
TO YOURSELF:

I WILL NEVER KEEP A SECRET THAT IS
HURTING ME OR THAT IS NOT RIGHT!

IF IT FEELS BAD OR WRONG,
I AM GOING TO SAY
SOMETHING TO GET HELP!

I AM BRAVE, SMART, STRONG, LOVED,
AND A SPECIAL GIFT TO THIS WORLD!

I MATTER!

I GOT THIS!

BAD SECRETS! NO, NOT FOR ME!

Printed in the United States
by Baker & Taylor Publisher Services